My Science Library

How Ecosystems Work

by Julie K. Lundgren

Science Content Editor:
Shirley Duke

Rourke
Educational Media

rourkeeducationalmedia.com

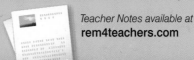

Teacher Notes available at
rem4teachers.com

Science Content Editor: Shirley Duke holds a bachelor's degree in biology and a master's degree in education from Austin College in Sherman, Texas. She taught science in Texas at all levels for twenty-five years before starting to write for children. Her science books include *You Can't Wear These Genes, Infections, Infestations, and Diseases, Enterprise STEM, Forces and Motion at Work, Environmental Disasters,* and *Gases.* She continues writing science books and also works as a science content editor.

www.rourkeeducationalmedia.com

Photo credits: Cover Mogens Trolle, Steve Byland; Table of Contents © Tischenko Irina; Page 4 © Igor Borodin; Page 4/5 © Eduard Kyslynskyy; Page 6 © Imageman; Page 6/7 © ehtesham; Page 8 © Diana Cochran Johnson, Bruce MacQueen, Joe Farah; Page 9 © Ashley Whitworth, Greg Hume, creativedoxfoto; Page 10/11 © Yvonne Pijnenburg-Schonewille; Page 12 © Pal Teravagimov; Page 13 © worldswildlifewonders, Pal Teravagimov, Roy Palmer, Mircea BEZERGHEANU, H.Damke, tagstiles.com - Sven Gruene, Andreas Gradin, Sascha Burkard, Fong Kam Yee, Cathy Keifer, Jakub Pavlinec, leungchopan, Ainars Aunins; Page 14 © Dr. Morley Read; © Page 14/15 © John A. Anderson; Page 16 © Dr. Morley Read, Studiotouch; Page 16/17 © Alexander Chelmodeev; Page 18 © U.S. Fish and Wildlife Service; Page 19 © U.S. Fish and Wildlife Service; © Page 18/19 © Danny E Hooks; Page 20 © Geoffrey Kuchera; Page 21 © Dusty Cline;

Editor: Kelli Hicks

My Science Library series produced by Nicola Stratford Design, Florida for Rourke Educational Media.

Library of Congress PCN Data

Lundgren, Julie K.
 How Ecosystems Work / Julie K. Lundgren.
   p. cm. -- (My Science Library)
 ISBN 978-1-61810-087-0 (Hard cover) (alk. paper)
 ISBN 978-1-61810-220-1 (Soft cover)
 Library of Congress Control Number: 2012930290

Rourke Educational Media
Printed in the United States of America,
North Mankato, Minnesota

rourkeeducationalmedia.com
customerservice@rourkeeducationalmedia.com
PO Box 643328 Vero Beach, Florida 32964

Table of Contents

Balanced System

A tree. A forest. A pond. An ocean. We can call each an **ecosystem**. We can describe the connections between the plants, animals, and **nonliving** things in ecosystems.

We can call a single tree and all that lives in its branches an ecosystem.

A plant takes up water from the soil. An animal eats a plant. Another animal finds shelter underground or in a tree hollow. Because of these connections, the living things **survive** and the ecosystem stays healthy. Together, they keep the system in balance.

What's the Difference?

Environment and habitat are words that talk about a place. An ecosystem describes all that happens in a place. For example, a desert environment receives less than 10 inches (25 centimeters) of rain or moisture each year. In parts of the desert of western Australia, mulga trees grow. Honeypot ants live in habitats containing mulga trees. What's happening in this habitat? Honeypot ants collect nectar from the mulga tree flowers and deliver it to special honeypot ants that act as living cupboards. They store the nectar in their **abdomens**. The rest of the ant colony feeds on these special ants when food is scarce. The native people of this area eat the honeypot ants, too.

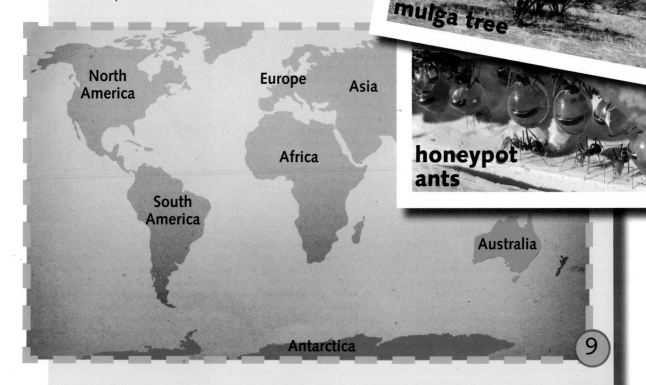

mulga tree

honeypot ants

North America

Europe

Asia

Africa

South America

Australia

Antarctica

Living Connections

Not every kind of animal can live in every ecosystem. Animals have **adaptations** that help them get what they need in order to survive in their ecosystem. Polar bears live in the Arctic and have fat and fur to protect them in temperatures that may dip to -70 degrees Fahrenheit (-57 degrees Celsius). They depend on breaks in the sea ice to hunt. They patrol the ocean's icy surface searching for the breathing holes of ringed seals, their favorite prey. Polar bears would not survive well in warm or iceless habitats.

Polar bears will wait patiently for a seal to pop its head up for air. When it does, a polar bear will grab it in its jaws and pull it up.

A **food web** describes who eats what in an ecosystem. It also shows how the Sun's **energy** moves through the ecosystem as animals eat. In a tropical rainforest, hundreds of kinds of shrubs and trees produce tasty leaves, seeds, and fruit. Fruit bats, sloths, insects, and other plant-eaters feed on them and, in turn, are eaten by carnivores. Harpy eagles, for example, regularly dine on sloths.

jaguar

Because animals use part of the energy they eat for living and store only a portion in their bodies, energy is lost as it moves up the food web. Food webs can support just a few top predators.

Cleaner shrimp pick food bits from their fishy customers' mouths without getting eaten. The shrimp get a meal and the fish get clean teeth.

What About Change?

Ecosystem changes can help keep it healthy. When a tree falls, it makes room for new, healthy trees to sprout.

Other changes are a normal part of life in that ecosystem, like the changing seasons.

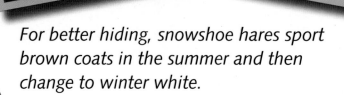

For better hiding, snowshoe hares sport brown coats in the summer and then change to winter white.

A break in the forest canopy allows sunlight to reach the forest floor and new sprouting plants.

People sometimes cause harmful changes. Animals' adaptations may no longer fit their environment. Animals may sicken or die. In California, red-legged frogs face threats from habitat loss, water pollution, overgrazing by cattle, mining, and other changes. The area where they can live successfully has decreased by seventy percent.

New housing threatens the habitat of red-legged frogs.

Forestry practices like clear-cutting, where every tree is removed, can affect forest habitat recovery.

Erosion is a common problem on beaches. People trample the native plants that hold the sand in place and build piers that change sea currents and wave patterns.

Trash, oil, and chemicals can wash from land into waterways.

Take Action!

Gather a group and clean up a natural area. Wear gloves to protect your hands. Let adults pick up sharp objects.

We must use great care to support the ecosystems around us. Changes to water, air, and land quality can reduce the ability of animals and plants to live successfully. A broken ecosystem has fewer kinds of plants and animals. It can take years to fix problems. How we live affects the balance of life in our environments. As citizens of Earth, we have a responsibility to care for our one and only planet.

Give a bird a home by hanging a birdhouse.

Show What You Know

1. Name three ecosystems, large or small.

2. In your ecosystem, what are connections that help you survive?

3. How can people live in balance with their ecosystems?

Glossary

abdomens (AB-duh-minz): in insects, the third and last section of their bodies, after the head and thorax

adaptations (ad-ap-TAY-shunz): changes in animals over time that help them live

ecosystem (EE-koh-siss-tuhm): a unit of nature that includes all the relationships between plants, animals, and the place they live

energy (EN-ur-jee): the body's ability to do the work needed to live

environment (en-VYE-ruhn-muhnt): the place around us, often meaning the natural world

food web (FOOD WEHB): in an ecosystem, all of the links between living things based on what they eat

habitats (HAB-uh-tats): homes for living things where they can find everything they need to live, including food and shelter

microorganisms (my-kroh-OR-gun-izmz): very tiny creatures that live in soil, water, or living things, and that are part of the food web in many ecosystems

nonliving (non-LIV-ing): without life, such as rocks, water, and minerals

nutrients (NOO-tree-uhnts): things needed for healthy growth, like vitamins and minerals

survive (sur-VIVE): continue to live, in spite of dangers

Index

Websites to Visit

www.buildyourwildself.com/

www.ecokids.ca/pub/kids_home.cfm

www.mbgnet.net/sets/index.htm

About the Author

Julie K. Lundgren has written more than 40 nonfiction books for children. She gets a kick out of sharing juicy facts about science, nature, and animals, especially if they are slightly disgusting! Through her work, she hopes kids will learn that Earth is an amazing place and young people can make a big difference in keeping our planet healthy. She lives in Minnesota with her family.

Ask The Author!
www.rem4students.com